CONTENTS

A SIGN OF WHAT'S COMING...

In his book The Last Word, author Thomas Nagel writes, 'I want atheism to be true, and I am made uneasy by the fact that some of the most intelligent and well informed people I know are religious believers. It isn't just that I don't believe in God and, naturally, hope that I'm right in my belief. It is that I hope there is no God. I don't want there to be a God, I don't want the universe to be like that.'

Why might someone 'hope there is no God'?

JOHN 20:30-31

1 What reasons does John give for writing his biography of Jesus?

2 John makes the identity of Jesus a major theme of his book. Who do you think Jesus might have been? How did you come to this conclusion?

In ancient Jewish thought, the Christ or Messiah was a promised leader of the Jewish nation, who would defeat the nation's enemies and lead the people into an era of peace and prosperity. In Jesus' day, different groups wanted to claim the idea of the Messiah for their own ends, often political and nationalistic.

HISTORICAL CONTEXT

The first public encounter that John presents us with is Jesus at a wedding with friends and family. Weddings in first-century Palestine were even more significant and lavish affairs than they are today. Marriage meant more than the joining of two individuals. A wedding marked the bride and groom's entrance as adults into their community. The celebrations usually lasted for at least a week. It was the responsibility of the groom to provide all that was necessary for such a hugely important social occasion.

JOHN 2:1-11

3 The wedding has run out of wine. How might the bride and groom feel if there was no wine at their wedding feast, especially in a shame/honour culture? What would be the impact on the whole celebration?

4 If the wine was finished, what would the wedding crowd conclude about the groom in particular? What would the bride's family conclude about their new son-in-law?

In the Hebrew Bible, wine represented joy, so its absence at a wedding would be disastrous. Jesus' reply to his mother isn't as stark as it first looks, but it is quite puzzling, especially when he says, 'My hour has not yet come' in verse 4. Jesus seems to be a man who knows his destiny and sees his whole life heading towards a particular moment.

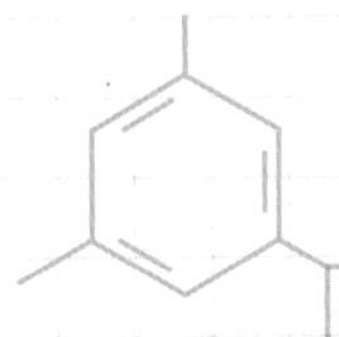

5 **Although Jesus is reluctant to step into the limelight at this point, why do you think he does something quite miraculous to help the couple?**

The six water jars were common items in a Jewish household. The water they contained was used for ceremonial washing, symbolising the need for moral purity before God could be approached. Each jar would contain 80–120 litres, the equivalent of 700–1,000 bottles of the best-quality vintage wine.

6 **Describe the Master of the Banquet's impression of the wine. How will this wine change the party?**

7 **What does the Master of the Banquet conclude about the groom? Does the groom deserve the credit? How would the bride and groom feel about what Jesus had done for them?**

Jesus has quietly rescued a wedding and saved a desperate couple from disgrace. But his disciples (or followers) saw that his actions pointed to something far more significant about him. They would be familiar with ancient Hebrew texts such as the following from the prophet Isaiah (c.700 BC):

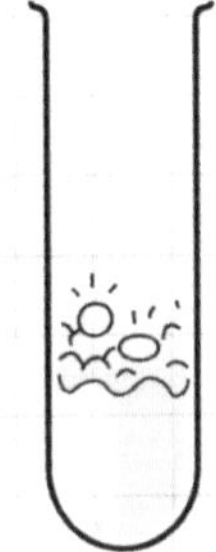

On this mountain the LORD Almighty will prepare a feast of rich food for all peoples, a banquet of aged wine – the best of meats and the finest of wines. On this mountain he will destroy the shroud that enfolds all peoples, the sheet that covers all nations; he will swallow up death for ever. The Sovereign LORD will wipe away the tears from all faces; he will remove his people's disgrace from all the earth. (Isaiah 25:6–8)

8 **Isaiah imagines what it will be like when the Lord Almighty, God, comes to the world. What will God do and for whom?**

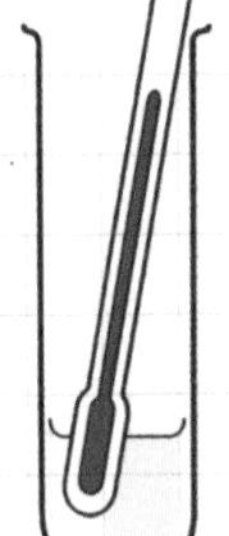

9 **Imagine that you are one of Jesus's disciples. You have grown up in a Jewish household, with a text like this ringing in your ears. Having just tasted the new wine from Jesus, what might you think about him?**

Isaiah is looking forward to a day when God himself will come to heal the world. Isaiah pictures this healing as the richest banquet imaginable. Other Hebrew texts speak about a particular person through whom God will do all this – the Messiah we were introduced to earlier. Could Jesus be the one who will fulfil all these hopes and dreams?

SO, WHAT DOES THIS MEAN FOR US?

Some people hope there is no God because they perceive religion to be life-diminishing. Given what John has said about Jesus bringing life, what does this first encounter suggest about the life Jesus gives to those who believe in him? What does this suggest about who he is?

DO YOU COME
HERE OFTEN?

'Resign yourself to the lifelong sadness
that comes from never being satisfied.'
– author Zadie Smith

Do you think it is possible to find lasting satisfaction, and if so, how?

Bb STUDY

HISTORICAL CONTEXT

In this encounter, Jesus does something that in his day would have been considered shocking. He speaks to a Samaritan woman. This might not sound like much, but in his culture, a religious man would never consider speaking to a woman in public. An ancient text said: 'Better is the wickedness of a man than a woman who does good; it is woman who brings shame and disgrace.' Jesus also ignores the deep racial and religious prejudice that Jews felt towards the Samaritans. Jews considered Samaritans 'heretics' because they combined some Jewish teaching with pagan practices.

We join Jesus at noon (the sixth hour, as it was the custom to count the hour from sunrise), in the sweltering midday heat, tired and thirsty.

JOHN 4:4-15

1 It was the custom for women to go together to the well to draw water in the cool of the morning. Why might this woman be drawing water alone and in the heat of the day?

2 Why is the woman so surprised that Jesus asks her for a drink, given that it was hot and he had nothing to draw water with?

3 How does Jesus describe what he can offer the woman? What do you think his deeper meaning might be? What does she need to do to get it?

4 How do you think she is responding to what Jesus is claiming to offer? Is she genuinely interested? Sceptical? Sarcastic? Flirtatious? Do you think her request in verse 15 is serious or cynical?

JOHN 4: 17-26

5 Jesus moves the conversation on to the subject of the woman's relationships. Why does she answer with only a half-truth in verse 17? How might this explain why she was at the well at noon and alone? How might other women have considered her?

6 How might she have been feeling after what Jesus has revealed he knows about her relationships? Why do you think Jesus exposed the reality of her life in this way?

Unsettled by his insight into her life, the woman starts to recognise that Jesus is at least a prophet. Her comments in verse 20 are not a change of subject; rather she is asking which temple she should go to in order to find forgiveness and be restored to God.

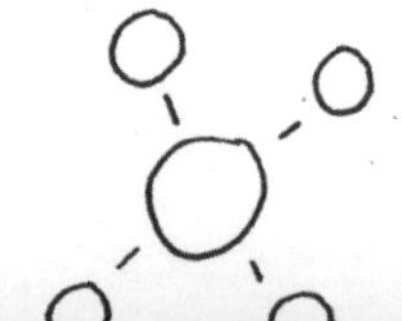

and everyone is going to him.'
[27]To this John replied, 'A person can receive only what is given them from heaven. [28]You yourselves can testify that I said, "I am not the Messiah but am sent ahead of him." [29]The bride belongs to the bridegroom. The friend who attends the bridegroom waits and listens for him, and is full of joy when he hears the bridegroom's voice. That joy is mine, and it is now complete. [30]He must become greater; I must become less.'h
[31]The one who comes from above is above all; the one who is from the earth belongs to the earth, and speaks as one from the earth. The one who comes from heaven is above all. [32]He testifies to what he has seen and heard, but no one accepts his testimony. [33]Whoever has accepted it has certified that God is truthful. [34]For the one whom God has sent speaks the words of God, for Godi gives the Spirit without limit. [35]The Father loves the Son and has placed everything in his hands. [36]Whoever believes in the Son has eternal life, but whoever rejects the Son will not see life, for God's wrath remains on them.

Jesus talks with a Samaritan woman

4 [4]Now he had to go through Samaria. [5]So he came to a town in Samaria called Sychar, near the plot of ground Jacob had given to his son Joseph. [6]Jacob's well was there, and Jesus, tired as he was from the journey, sat down by the well. It was about noon.
[7]When a Samaritan woman came to draw water, Jesus said to her, 'Will you give me a drink?' [8](His disciples had gone into the town to buy food.)
[9]The Samaritan woman said to him, 'You are a Jew and I am a Samaritan woman. How can you ask me for a drink?' (For Jews do not associate with Samaritans.)
[10]Jesus answered her, 'If you knew the gift of God and who it is that asks you for a drink, you would have asked him and he would have given you living water.'
[11]'Sir,' the woman said, 'you have nothing to draw with and the well is deep. Where can you get this living water? [12]Are you greater than our father Jacob, who gave us the well and drank from it himself, as did also his sons and his livestock?'
[13]Jesus answered, 'Everyone who drinks this water will be thirsty again, [14]but whoever drinks the water I give them will never thirst. Indeed, the water I give them will become in them a spring of water welling up to eternal life.'
[15]The woman said to him, 'Sir, give me this water so that I won't get thirsty and have to keep coming here to draw water.'
[16]He told her, 'Go, call your husband and come back.'
[17]'I have no husband,' she replied.
Jesus said to her, 'You are right when you say you have no husband. [18]The fact is, you have had five husbands, and the man you now have is not your husband. What you have just said is quite true.'
[19]'Sir,' the woman said, 'I can see that you are a prophet. [20]Our ancestors worshipped on this mountain, but you Jews claim that the place where we must worship is in Jerusalem.'
[21]'Woman,' Jesus replied, 'believe me, a time is coming when you will worship the Father neither on this mountain nor in Jerusalem. [22]You Samaritans worship what you do not know; we worship what we do know, for salvation is from the Jews. [23]Yet a time is coming and has now come when the true worshippers will worship the Father in the Spirit and in truth, for they are the kind of worshippers the Father seeks. [24]God is spirit, and his worshippers must worship in the Spirit and in truth.'
[25]The woman said, 'I know that Messiah' (called Christ) 'is coming. When he comes, he will explain everything to us.'
[26]Then Jesus declared, 'I, the one speaking to you – I am he.'

The disciples rejoin Jesus

[27]Just then his disciples returned and were surprised to find him talking with a woman. But no one asked, 'What do you want?' or 'Why are you talking with her?'

[28]Then, leaving her water jar, the woman went back to the town and said to the people,

...

Many Samaritans believe

[39]Many of the Samaritans from that town believed in him because of the woman's testimony, 'He told me everything I've ever done.' [40]So when the Samaritans came to him, they urged him to stay with them, and he stayed two days. [41]And because of his words many more became believers.

[42]They said to the woman, 'We no longer believe just because of what you said; now we have heard for ourselves, and we know that this man really is the Saviour of the world.'

Jesus heals an official's son

[43]After the two days he left for Galilee. [44](Now Jesus himself had pointed out that a prophet has no honour in his own country.) [45]When he arrived in Galilee, the Galileans welcomed him. They had seen all that he had done in Jerusalem at the Passover Festival, for they also had been there.

[46]Once more he visited Cana in Galilee, where he had turned the water into wine. And there was a certain royal official whose son lay ill at Capernaum. [47]When this man heard that Jesus had arrived in Galilee from Judea, he went to him and begged him to come and heal his son, who was close to death.

[48]'Unless you people see signs and wonders,' Jesus told him, 'you will never believe.'

[49]The royal official said, 'Sir, come down before my child dies.'

[50]'Go,' Jesus replied, 'your son will live.'

The man took Jesus at his word and departed. [51]While he was still on the way, his servants met him with the news that his boy was living. [52]When he enquired as to the time when his son got better, they said to him, 'Yesterday, at one in the afternoon, the fever left him.'

[53]Then the father realised that this was the exact time at which Jesus had said to him, 'Your son will live.' So he and his whole household believed.

[54]This was the second sign Jesus performed after coming from Judea to Galilee.

The healing at the pool

5 Some time later, Jesus went up to Jerusalem for one of the Jewish festivals. [2]Now there is in Jerusalem near the Sheep Gate a pool, which in Aramaic is called Bethesdaa and which is surrounded by five covered colonnades. [3]Here a great number of disabled people used to lie – the blind, the lame, the paralysed. [4]b [5]One who was there had been an invalid for thirty-eight years. [6]When Jesus saw him lying there and learned that he had been in this condition for a long time, he asked him, 'Do you want to get well?' [7]'Sir,' the invalid replied, 'I have no one to help me into the pool when the water is stirred. While I am trying to get in, someone else goes down ahead of me.' [8]Then Jesus said to him, 'Get up! Pick up your mat and walk.' [9]At once the man was cured; he picked up his mat and walked.

The day on which this took place was a Sabbath, [10]and so the Jewish leaders said to the man who had been healed, 'It is the Sabbath; the law forbids you to carry your mat.'

7 Rephrase the main statements of Jesus' response to the woman in verses 21–24. What might he mean?

8 In verse 26, Jesus claims to be the 'Messiah'. Looking back, what does he claim to bring? What is the gift of God he talks about in verse 10?

JOHN 4: 27-28, 39-42

9 Describe the reaction of the disciples when they return to the well in verse 27. Why do they react in this way?

10 Given all that we know about this woman, what strikes you as so surprising about her actions in verses 28–29? How do you think she is feeling now? Why?

11 According to verses 39–42, what do the people of the town come to believe, and what has persuaded them?

SO, WHAT DOES THIS MEAN FOR US?

A sense of emptiness is a common human experience. Rock star and humanitarian ambassador Bob Geldof was once asked whether he had found satisfaction: 'Not at all. I don't know what that would mean. I am unfulfilled as a human being. Otherwise, why are these large holes here [thumping his chest]. Everything I do is because I am frightened of being bored, because I know what is down there in those holes. I am frightened of it, it makes me depressed.'

Actor and comedian Russell Brand describes the achievement of celebrity as 'like being presented with this most glorious meal and then when you eat it there's no taste, there's no succour, there's no nutrition. It's ... tiresome.'

How do you respond to what Bob Geldof and Russell Brand say? Are you optimistic or cynical about the possibility of finding satisfaction?

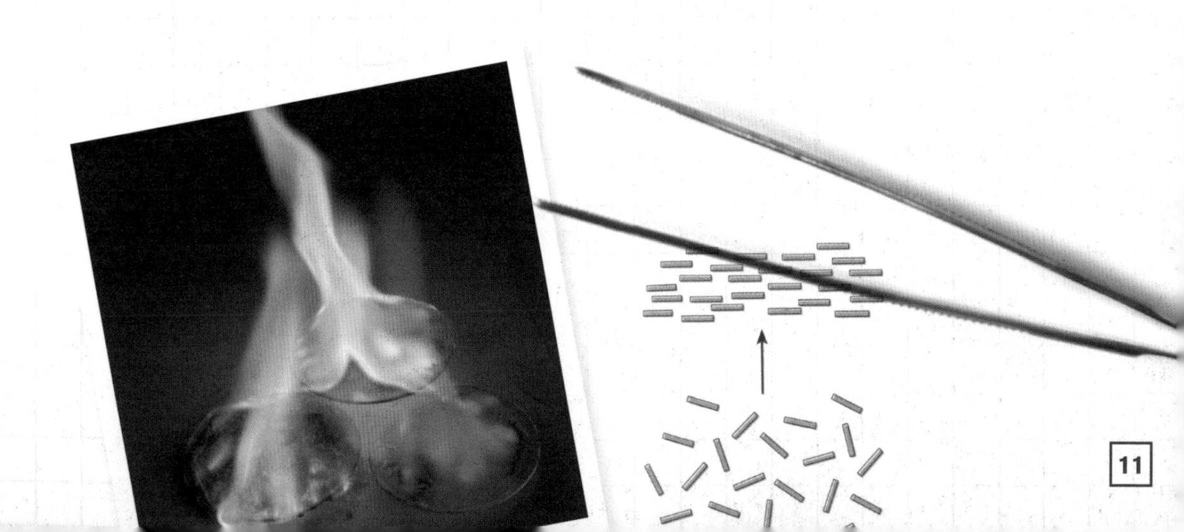

WARNING

Cc
STUDY

BLIND FAITH

'The emotional dog wags the rational tail.' The social psychologist Jonathan Haidt argues that we are less rational than we think and, more typically, we see only what we want to see and believe what we want to be true.

Do you think this applies especially to religious people, or is it true of all of us?

HISTORICAL CONTEXT

Opinions about Jesus are becoming sharply divided. Is he from God or is he a deluded troublemaker? The Pharisees, strict adherents to the Jewish religious law, were angry with him. For them, Jesus didn't keep the Sabbath, a day on which Jews were to refrain from any form of work in order to worship. But Jesus had healed someone on the Sabbath, which they considered a break in the Sabbath regulations. They were so angry with Jesus that in the previous chapter they tried to murder him.

In this encounter, Jesus rejects the popular notion that a man's blindness was the result of his own or his parents' sin. Jesus heals the man on the Sabbath and is once again embroiled in controversy.

JOHN 9:1-7

1 Describe what life would be like for someone born blind – practically, socially, emotionally. Note the hints in verses 1 and 8.

2 What would sight mean for the man? How might he have felt as he walked to the pool? What might he have been thinking as he came back to the place where he was once forced to beg?

3 How does this miracle relate to Jesus claiming to be the light of the world? What does it suggest about the life Jesus claims to offer?

JOHN 9:8-23

4 Why do you think the man's neighbours respond as they do? Why would they take him to the Pharisees in verses 8–13?

5 The Pharisees now enter the scene. Why can't they agree about what has happened, despite the clear testimony of the man? Read verses 13–17. What assumptions are guiding their conclusions?

6 Why are the man's parents now brought in? How do they respond in verses 18–23, and why?

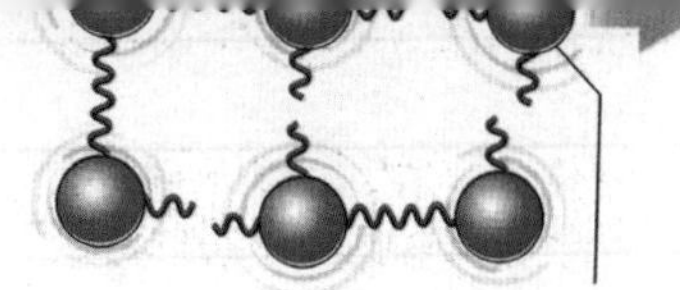

JOHN 9:24-34

7 Why do you think the Pharisees react as they do to the man's testimony? Are they interested in 'the truth'?

8 How does the man respond to the accusations and insults of the Pharisees? What points does he make in verses 30–33?

JOHN 9:35-41

9 Why do you think Jesus seeks out the man?

10 In the last few hours, this man experiences a radical re-evaluation of who he thinks Jesus is. How has his opinion changed in verses 11, 17 and 38, and what conclusion has he reached about Jesus' identity?

For the first time in this encounter, the man sees Jesus with his physical eyes and worships him. The man's journey from blindness to sight parallels his spiritual journey as he follows the evidence and comes to see who Jesus truly is. The term 'son of man' could just refer to another human being, but the Hebrew Scriptures use the term to describe a person with God-like characteristics.

11 This encounter began with the assumption that the blind man was sinful. It ends in an incredibly unexpected way, with Jesus describing the Pharisees in this manner. What are they guilty of? What keeps them from accepting the conclusion to which the evidence points?

SO, WHAT DOES THIS MEAN FOR US?

Jesus makes bold claims about himself in this passage. In claiming to be the 'light of the world', he insists that we are all in darkness without him. In the Hebrew Bible, worship was reserved for God alone, so by receiving the man's worship, Jesus equates himself with God.

Oxford academic and author CS Lewis wrote about Jesus: 'You can shut him up as a fool, you can spit on him and kill him as a demon; or you can fall at his feet and call him Lord and God. But let us not come up with any patronizing nonsense about his being a great human teacher. He has not left that open to us. He didn't intend to.'

Why do you think we are more comfortable thinking about Jesus as a great teacher, but perhaps choose to reject the kinds of claims he makes about himself in this encounter?

DEAD MAN WALKING

This session explores the painful topic of death.

Why do you think it is a subject we so often avoid talking openly about?

HISTORICAL CONTEXT

Jesus has made some bold claims about himself, not least that he is the Messiah, God's saviour of the world. In the previous chapter, he claimed to be God's Son. The Jewish leaders are so outraged, they respond with murderous intent: 'We are not trying to stone you for any good work, but for blasphemy ... because you, a mere man, claim to be God' (John 10:33). They understood Jesus to mean that he claimed to share the same nature of God, whom he called his Father.

Jesus is now confronted with the death of a very close friend. Can he offer any hope in the face of death? Will he confirm his incredible claims to be God in human form? What evidence is there to suggest that we take his claim to be the saviour of the world seriously?

JOHN 11:1-16

1 What relationship did Jesus have with Lazarus and his family (see verses 3 and 5)? Why do you think they would send for Jesus?

2 When Jesus hears about Lazarus' illness, what is so surprising about his response? Read verses 5–6. What do the disciples fear will happen?

3 At what point does Jesus decide to go and see Lazarus? How do the disciples misunderstand what he says in verses 11–16?

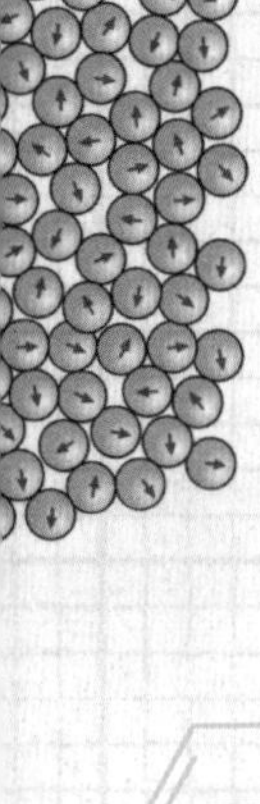

4 It would seem utterly pointless for Jesus to walk for four days in order to see Lazarus now. What reason does Jesus give to explain his delay in verses 4 and 15?

In the Hebrew Scriptures, 'glory' referred to the visible manifestation of God, usually in the form of radiance and splendour. Jesus is saying that through what will happen at the home of Lazarus, the disciples are going to see that Jesus shares the same glory, the same nature as God himself. His deliberate delay in going to Bethany is for this purpose.

JOHN 11:17-27

5 Describe the scene that confronted Jesus when he arrived at the home of Lazarus. How do you think Mary and Martha were feeling? What do you think they expected Jesus to do?

6 What does Jesus say to Martha in response to her grief? Read verses 23–25. How does Jesus' response both confirm and challenge what she believes? According to Jesus, how is it possible for anyone to be confident of life after death?

JOHN 11: 28-46

7 Why does Mary eventually go out to meet Jesus? What strikes you most about Jesus' response to her grief?

8 Jesus is said to be 'deeply moved' in verse 33 and 'troubled' in verse 38 – literally 'angry' and 'outraged' in the original language. His grief is understandable, but why do you think he is angry?

9 What are the crowd thinking? What are they expecting to happen in verses 36–37? What is Martha expecting in verse 39?

10 Describe what Jesus does in verses 43–44. How does this relate to his claim about himself in verses 25–26?

11 Read verses 41–42. According to Jesus, how does he want people to respond to what they have seen? How do they actually respond in verses 45–48?

Jesus said that he deliberately delayed going to see and help Lazarus. His intention was that through what he would do, people would see that he shares the same nature as God. If Jesus is God, then what aspects of God's nature are revealed here?

SO, WHAT DOES THIS MEAN FOR US?

After being diagnosed with terminal cancer, Apple founder Steve Jobs said: 'I can now say this to you with a bit more certainty than when death was a useful but purely intellectual concept. No one wants to die. Even people who want to go to heaven don't want to die to get there. And yet, death is the destination we all share. No one has ever escaped it.'

Although we do at times feel immortal, death is the destination we all share. Does Jesus' claim to be 'the resurrection and the life' give you hope? Why or why not?

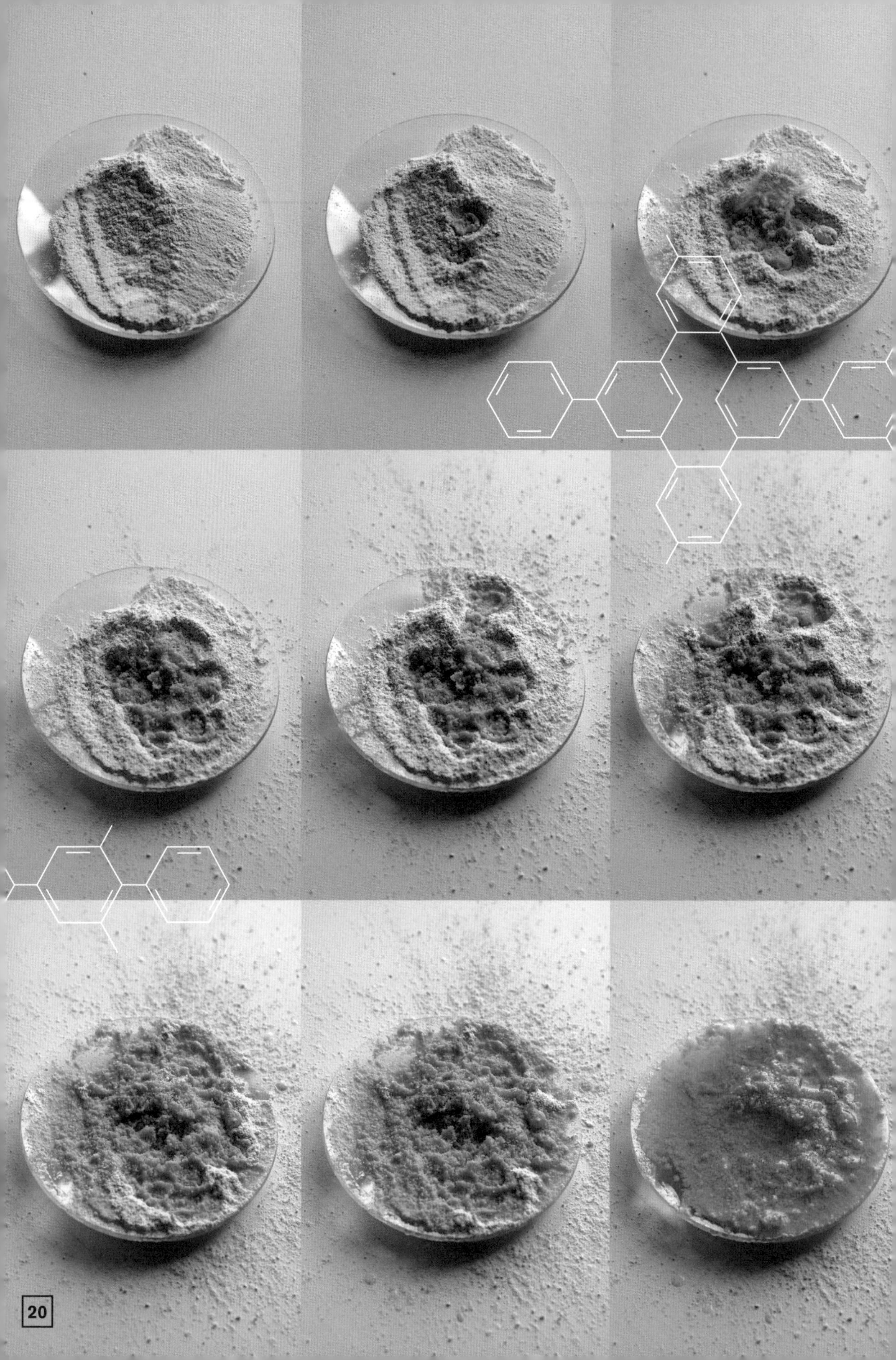

Ee STUDY	THE GREAT EXCHANGE

Russian novelist and human rights campaigner Alexander Solzhenitsyn considered the hypothetical possibility of ridding the world of evil people. He eventually came to the conclusion that this would be impossible: 'The line dividing good and evil cuts through the heart of every human being. And who is willing to destroy a piece of his own heart?'

To what extent do you agree with this description of humanity?

Ee
STUDY

HISTORICAL CONTEXT

The religious leaders have resolved to put Jesus to death for blasphemy, because Jesus claimed to be the divine saviour of the world. An opportunity arrived when Judas, one of Jesus' disciples, agreed to betray him. In the hours before this account, Jesus had been arrested and evidence fabricated in order to condemn him. Only the occupying Roman authorities could inflict the death penalty, so the Roman governor Pontius Pilate had to be persuaded of Jesus' guilt.

The religious leaders knew that Pilate would have no interest in being dragged into their religious quarrel. In order to secure Jesus' condemnation, they try to persuade Pilate that the preacher from Galilee should be executed on the grounds of treason.

JOHN 19:1-16

1 **Describe the attitude of the soldiers towards Jesus. Why are they mocking him?**

2 **What does Pilate emphasise about Jesus as a result of his interrogation in verses 4, 6 and 12?**

3 **Why does Pilate become afraid when he hears the charges brought against Jesus in verses 7–8?**

4 **Jesus is before the man who has power to execute him. What strikes you about Pilate and Jesus in their interchange in verses 9–11?**

5 **Read verses 12–16. Pilate hopes to set Jesus free. How are the religious leaders finally able to persuade Pilate to pronounce the sentence of execution on Jesus?**

JOHN 19:17-27

In one short sentence, John tells us that Jesus was crucified. Yet crucifixion was one of the most horrific punishments imaginable. It was used as the ultimate deterrent to rebellion against Rome. Notices that gave reason for crucifixion were therefore nailed above those being executed. Jewish law added to the humiliation of crucifixion by stating that anyone killed in this way was considered to be cursed by God.

6 **What was the charge upon which Pilate agreed to the execution of Jesus? Read verses 19–22. Why were the religious leaders so upset by this?**

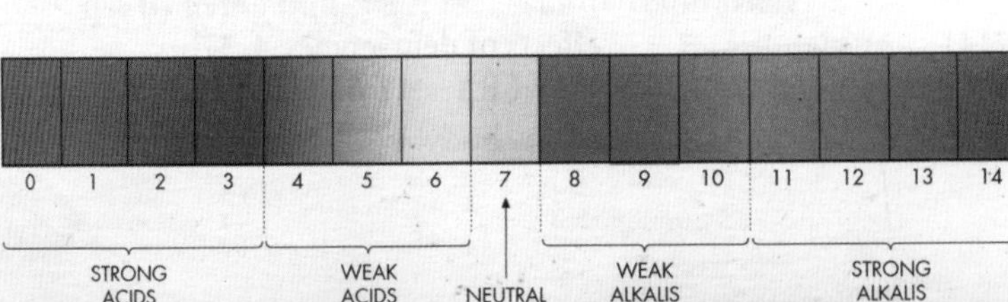

Jesus sentenced to be crucified

19 [1]Then Pilate took Jesus and had him flogged. [2]The soldiers twisted together a crown of thorns and put it on his head. They clothed him in a purple robe [3]and went up to him again and again, saying, 'Hail, king of the Jews!' And they slapped him in the face.

[4]Once more Pilate came out and said to the Jews gathered there, 'Look, I am bringing him out to you to let you know that I find no basis for a charge against him.' [5]When Jesus came out wearing the crown of thorns and the purple robe, Pilate said to them, 'Here is the man!'

[6]As soon as the chief priests and their officials saw him, they shouted, 'Crucify! Crucify!'

But Pilate answered, 'You take him and crucify him. As for me, I find no basis for a charge against him.'

[7]The Jewish leaders insisted, 'We have a law, and according to that law he must die, because he claimed to be the Son of God.'

[8]When Pilate heard this, he was even more afraid, [9]and he went back inside the palace. 'Where do you come from?' he asked Jesus, but Jesus gave him no answer. [10]'Do you refuse to speak to me?' Pilate said. 'Don't you realise I have power either to free you or to crucify you?'

[11]Jesus answered, 'You would have no power over me if it were not given to you from above. Therefore the one who handed me over to you is guilty of a greater sin.'

[12]From then on, Pilate tried to set Jesus free, but the Jewish leaders kept shouting, 'If you let this man go, you are no friend of Caesar. Anyone who claims to be a king opposes Caesar.'

[13]When Pilate heard this, he brought Jesus out and sat down on the judge's seat at a place known as the Stone Pavement (which in Aramaic is Gabbatha). [14]It was the day of Preparation of the Passover; it was about noon.

'Here is your king,' Pilate said to the Jews. [15]But they shouted, 'Take him away! Take him away! Crucify him!'

'Shall I crucify your king?' Pilate asked. 'We have no king but Caesar,' the chief priests answered.

[16]Finally Pilate handed him over to them to be crucified.

The crucifixion of Jesus

So the soldiers took charge of Jesus. [17]Carrying his own cross, he went out to the place of the Skull (which in Aramaic is called Golgotha). [18]There they crucified him, and with him two others – one on each side and Jesus in the middle.

[19]Pilate had a notice prepared and fastened to the cross. It read: Jesus of nazareth, the king of the jews. [20]Many of the Jews read this sign, for the place where Jesus was crucified was near the city, and the sign was written in Aramaic, Latin and Greek. [21]The chief priests of the Jews protested to Pilate, 'Do not write "The King of the Jews", but that this man claimed to be king of the Jews.'

[22]Pilate answered, 'What I have written, I have written.'

[23]When the soldiers crucified Jesus, they took his clothes, dividing them into four shares, one for each of them, with the undergarment remaining. This garment was seamless, woven in one piece from top to bottom. [24]'Let's not tear it,' they said to one another. 'Let's decide by lot who will get it.'

This happened that the scripture might be fulfilled that said, 'They divided my clothes among them and cast lots for my garment.'

So this is what the soldiers did.

[25]Near the cross of Jesus stood his mother, his mother's sister, Mary the wife of Clopas, and Mary Magdalene. [26]When Jesus saw his mother there, and the disciple whom he loved standing near by, he said to her,

'Woman, here is your son,' [27]and to the disciple, 'Here is your mother.' From that time on, this disciple took her into his home.

The death of Jesus

[28]Later, knowing that everything had now been finished, and so that Scripture would be fulfilled, Jesus said, 'I am thirsty.' [29]A jar of wine vinegar was there, so they soaked a sponge in it, put the sponge on a stalk of the hyssop plant, and lifted it to Jesus' lips. [30]When he had received the drink, Jesus said, 'It is finished.' With that, he bowed his head and gave up his spirit.

[31]Now it was the day of Preparation, and the next day was to be a special Sabbath. Because the Jewish leaders did not want the bodies left on the crosses during the Sabbath, they asked Pilate to have the legs broken and the bodies taken down. [32]The soldiers therefore came and broke the legs of the first man who had been crucified with Jesus, and then those of the other. [33]But when they came to Jesus and found that he was already dead, they did not break his legs. [34]Instead, one of the soldiers pierced Jesus' side with a spear, bringing a sudden flow of blood and water. [35]The man who saw it has given testimony, and his testimony is true. He knows that he tells the truth, and he testifies so that you also may believe. [36]These things happened so that the scripture would be fulfilled: 'Not one of his bones will be broken,' [37]and, as another scripture says, 'They will look on the one they have pierced.'

The burial of Jesus

[38]Later, Joseph of Arimathea asked Pilate for the body of Jesus. Now Joseph was a disciple of Jesus, but secretly because he feared the Jewish leaders. With Pilate's permission, he came and took the body away. [39]He was accompanied by Nicodemus, the man who earlier had visited Jesus at night. Nicodemus brought a mixture of myrrh and aloes, about thirty-five kilograms. [40]Taking Jesus' body, the two of them wrapped it, with the spices, in strips of linen. This was in accordance with Jewish burial customs. [41]At the place where Jesus was crucified, there was a garden, and in the garden a new tomb, in which no one had ever been laid. [42]Because it was the Jewish day of Preparation and since the tomb was near by, they laid Jesus there.

The empty tomb

20 [1]Early on the first day of the week, while it was still dark, Mary Magdalene went to the tomb and saw that the stone had been removed from the entrance. [2]So she came running to Simon Peter and the other disciple, the one Jesus loved, and said, 'They have taken the Lord out of the tomb, and we don't know where they have put him!'

[3]So Peter and the other disciple started for the tomb. [4]Both were running, but the other disciple outran Peter and reached the tomb first. [5]He bent over and looked in at the strips of linen lying there but did not go in. [6]Then Simon Peter came along behind him and went straight into the tomb. He saw the strips of linen lying there, [7]as well as the cloth that had been wrapped round Jesus' head. The cloth was still lying in its place, separate from the linen. [8]Finally the other disciple, who had reached the tomb first, also went inside. He saw and believed. [9](They still did not understand from Scripture that Jesus had to rise from the dead.) [10]Then the disciples went back to where they were staying.

Jesus appears to Mary Magdalene

[11]Now Mary stood outside the tomb crying. As she wept, she bent over to look into the tomb [12]and saw two angels in white, seated where Jesus' body had been, one at the head and the other at the foot.

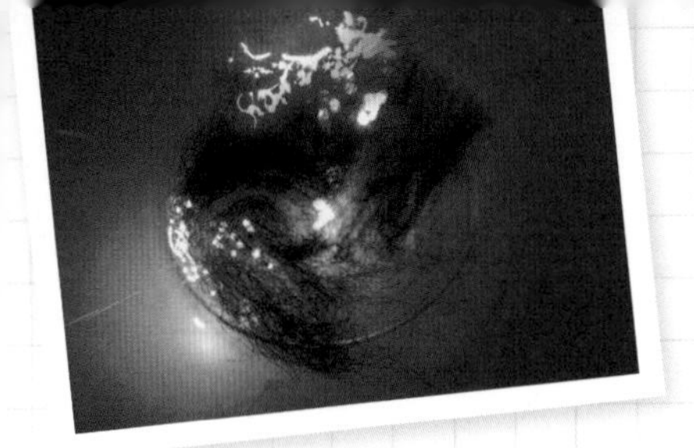

JOHN 19:28–42

7 **Everything suggests that Jesus is utterly ruined. Yet what hints are there that Jesus believes he is still truly in control (see verses 28, 30)?**

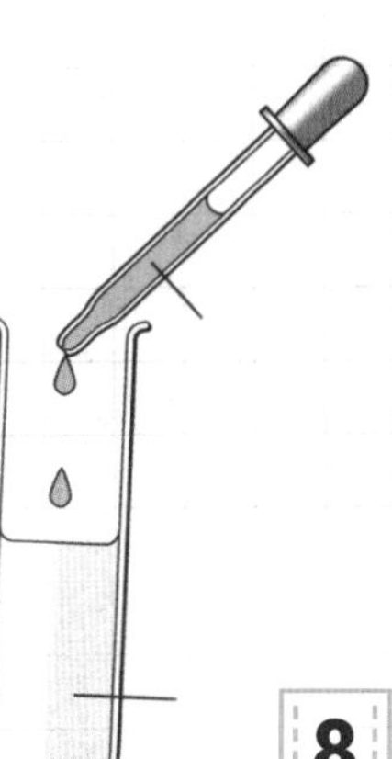

As John reports the events of Jesus' crucifixion, he continually refers to the fulfilment of Old Testament predictions of what would happen to the Messiah and what it would mean for the world. Isaiah describes the events of the crucifixion:

He was despised and rejected by mankind, a man of suffering, and familiar with pain. Like one from whom people hide their faces he was despised, and we held him in low esteem. Surely he took up our pain and bore our suffering, yet we considered him punished by God, stricken by him, and afflicted. But he was pierced for our transgressions, he was crushed for our iniquities; the punishment that brought us peace was on him, and by his wounds we are healed. We all, like sheep, have gone astray, each of us has turned to our own way; and the LORD has laid on him the iniquity of us all. Isaiah 53:3–6 (700 BC)

8 **How do these words reflect what Jesus is experiencing? According to Isaiah, what problem does the Messiah come to address? How would he achieve it?**

9 **Before he dies, Jesus shouts out, 'It is finished.' This phrase was written across receipts when a debt had been paid and nothing further was owed. What do you think Jesus believes his death on the cross is achieving?**

10 **Nicodemus, a distinguished religious teacher, embalms Jesus' body with a huge quantity of spices. Such an amount would be reserved for kings. Why is it so surprising that Nicodemus wishes to give Jesus such a burial?**

SO, WHAT DOES THIS MEAN FOR US?

Author Tim Keller understands the cross to be the unique element of Christianity in which Jesus substitutes himself for us, paying for our guilt, rather than us paying ourselves. He writes, 'The founders of every other major religion essentially came as teachers, not as saviours. They came to say: 'Do this and you will find the divine.' But Jesus came essentially as a saviour rather than a teacher (though he was that as well). Jesus says 'I am the divine come to you, to do what you could not do for yourselves.' The Christian message is that we are saved not by our record, but by Christ's record.'

Given what you have learned about the death of Jesus, is Tim Keller right? Is the essence of the cross one of salvation, in which God pays for us?

EXPLOSIVE

SEE FOR YOURSELF

Confirmation bias is the tendency to interpret new evidence as confirmation of one's existing beliefs or theories. Why do you think people can sometimes be resistant to questioning and changing their existing beliefs?

What kinds of evidence would you need in order to change your mind about something?

HISTORICAL CONTEXT

After Jesus' public execution, his followers went into hiding. Joseph of Arimathea and Nicodemus laid the body in Joseph's family tomb. The custom was to wrap the corpse and cover it with spices, then leave it sealed in the tomb until the flesh had rotted away. About a year later, the skeletal remains would have been recovered and transferred to a second burial place (an ossuary). There the story of Jesus would have ended – a dead Messiah was no Messiah at all.

But here we are, still talking about him...

JOHN 20:1-9

1 Imagine how the disciples must have felt in the days after Jesus' death. How might they now reflect on their last three years with Jesus? What might their thoughts be about their future?

2 Mary goes to the tomb and finds the large stone, used to prevent anyone from stealing the body, rolled away from the entrance. What conclusion does she reach about what has happened to the body?

3 Peter and the other disciple arrive at the tomb. They find that the body has gone, just as Mary had described. What are the possible explanations for this?

4 What do you think the other disciple saw in the tomb that convinced him that something more was going on here than simply a grave robbery?

5 Mary remains standing outside the tomb. What is the cause of her distress? Read verses 11–15. What possibilities is she open to? What convinced her that Jesus was alive with her?

6 The pagan philosopher Celsus ridiculed Christians for having a 'hysterical woman' as their key witness of the resurrection. He will not have been alone, since at this time, women were not acceptable as legal witnesses. What does it suggest about Jesus that he chose to present himself alive to Mary first? Does this suggest anything about the reliability of John's account itself?

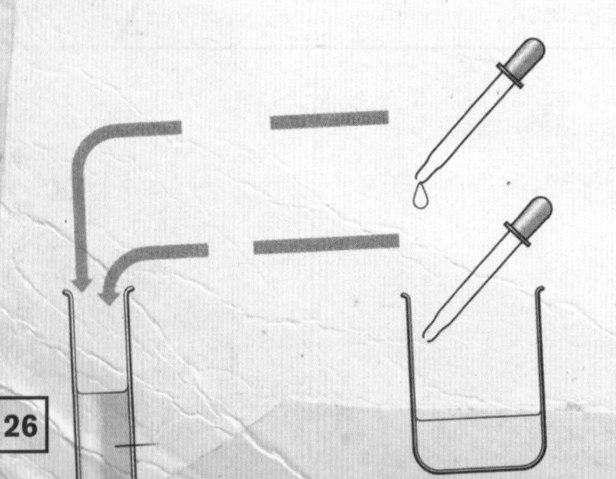